NO TRUMP
PLAY

RAYMOND BROCK
Foreword by BOBBY WOLFF

HOW TO PLAY BRIDGE

NTC
NTC Publishing Group

Library of Congress Cataloging-In-Publication Data is on file at the United States Library of Congress

Published by NTC Publishing Group
A division of NTC/Contemporary Publishing Group, Inc.
Copyright © 1998 by Raymond Brock
4255 West Touhy Avenue, Lincolnwood (Chicago), Illinois 60646-1975 U.S.A.

Printed in Singapore
International Standard Book Number:
0-8442-0078-6

foreword

Bridge is a game enjoyed by many millions of players all over the world.

In these days of rising commercial pressures, increasing leisure and greater longevity, bridge has the potential to break down social and ethnic barriers and to keep the wheels of the brain turning in both the old and the young. Apart from that, bridge at whatever level is a very inexpensive game, all you need to play is a flat surface that the four players can sit round with a pack of cards and, of course, an understanding as to how to play the game.

It is for these reasons that I am particularly pleased to welcome the 'How to Play Bridge' series which has been specially designed to make the game easy to follow for beginners, no matter what their age. I believe that you will find the whole series well presented and particularly easy to read.

Bobby Wolff
Dallas, Texas
March 1997

contents

introduction

Beginners do not like to play contracts without a trump suit because they worry that the opponents may be able to run a long suit. For similar reasons many players avoid opening 1NT with a weak doubleton. However, this concern is exaggerated. If partner bids game, maybe he has good cards in the suit; and in a partscore what does it matter if the opponents cash some tricks in the weak suit since we will make the rest of the tricks.

No trump contracts are in fact easier to play than suit contracts – there are fewer choices! You don't have to worry about whether to ruff, or about your winners being ruffed by the opponents, or about being overruffed, or trump promotions, or any other concerns that relate directly to a trump suit.

This book is written as a series of problems followed by a question and answer explanation of the thought processes that go into deciding upon the correct line of play. The four hands are given, followed by the bidding. The system in use throughout the book is Standard American with a strong (16-18) no trump and five-card majors. After the bidding there is the opening lead. Pause at this point and think about the hand yourself. Decide upon your line of play before reading on. Your understanding of the point in each hand will be helped if you lay out the deal with a pack of cards and play the hand through.

Before you start, a word of explanation about some terms used throughout the book to describe the three categories of winner:

1 *'Top tricks'* – aces; kings in suits where you already have aces; queens in suits where you already have the ace and king, etc.

2 *'Delayed tricks'* – certain tricks but you first need to knock out one or more of the opponents' high cards. KQx is one 'delayed trick', as is QJ10.

3 *'Possible tricks'* – cards that may or may not be tricks. There are two types. Firstly, there are the 'possible' tricks that depend upon the distribution of the opponents' cards. For example, if you hold A432 in one hand and K765 in the other you will make three tricks in the suit only if the opponents' cards are divided 3-2. If either opponent holds four (or five) cards in the suit, you will only make your ace and king. Secondly, there are the 'possible' tricks that depend upon the presence of one or more specified cards in the hand of a particular opponent:

♠ K8

	N	
W		E
	S	

♠ 62

You lead the two and when West follows with the five play the king from dummy. If West has the ace the king will be a trick, but if East holds the ace he will play it on the king and you will not make a trick in the suit.

A variation on the theme:

♠ A64

	N	
W		E
	S	

♠ QJ10

Here you hope that West has the king and you lead the queen. If West has the king you will make three tricks without losing any whilst if East has the king you will still make two tricks, the ace and the jack, but you will have lost one trick in the process. This play is known as a finesse, see pages 40–51.

deal 1
simple suit establishment

This first hand is very easy to get you off to a good start. It will help you to get used to the style.

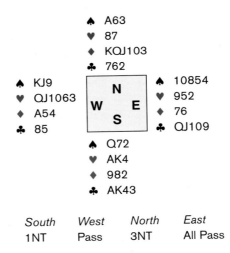

```
                    ♠ A63
                    ♥ 87
                    ♦ KQJ103
                    ♣ 762
     ♠ KJ9                        ♠ 10854
     ♥ QJ1063        N            ♥ 952
     ♦ A54        W     E         ♦ 76
     ♣ 85            S            ♣ QJ109
                    ♠ Q72
                    ♥ AK4
                    ♦ 982
                    ♣ AK43
```

South	West	North	East
1NT	Pass	3NT	All Pass

West leads the queen of hearts against your 3NT.
Plan the play.

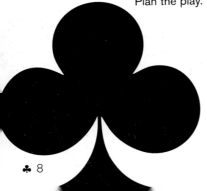

How many winners do you have?

In top tricks you have: 1 in spades, 2 in hearts and 2 in clubs = 5
In delayed tricks you have: 4 in diamonds
In total you have 9 sure winners.

How many times will you need to lose the lead to establish your nine tricks?

Just once, when you knock out the ace of diamonds.

What can go wrong?

In this instance nothing. You have a double stopper in hearts and as soon as you have knocked out the ace of diamonds you will be able to take 9 tricks.

The play

Trick 1: Win the king of hearts.
Tricks 2-4: Play diamonds. West will win the third round with the ace.
Trick 5: Win West's jack of hearts with your ace.
Tricks 6-13: Cross to dummy's ace of spades, cash your two remaining diamonds followed by your ace and king of clubs for a total of nine tricks.

The first thing to do on every single hand is count your tricks.

deal 2
unscrambling your tricks

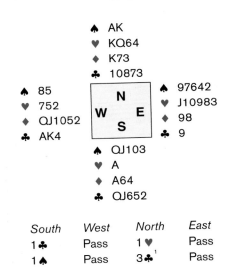

```
              ♠ AK
              ♥ KQ64
              ♦ K73
              ♣ 10873
♠ 85                         ♠ 97642
♥ 752          N             ♥ J10983
♦ QJ1052    W     E          ♦ 98
♣ AK4          S             ♣ 9
              ♠ QJ103
              ♥ A
              ♦ A64
              ♣ QJ652
```

South	West	North	East
1♣	Pass	1♥	Pass
1♠	Pass	3♣[1]	Pass
3NT	All Pass		

[1] forcing

West leads the queen of diamonds against your 3NT. Plan the play.

How many winners do you have?

In top tricks you have: 4 in spades, 3 in hearts and
2 in diamonds = 9
In delayed tricks you have: 3 in clubs
In total you have 12 sure winners.

What can go wrong?

You have nine top tricks plus three
more potential winners in clubs.
Surely you should make your
contract easily. On this hand
you have to be very careful. If
you win the lead and play
a club, West will win and
clear the diamonds.
You will find that you
can no longer cash
your nine top winners
because of insuperable
entry problems. If you win the
king of diamonds to cash your
nine sure tricks you will find that
you can no longer make your
contract. Try it. The order in which you
cash your tricks on this hand is very
important.

The play

Trick 1: Win the ace of diamonds.
Tricks 2-3: Cash the ace and king of spades.

Trick 4: Play a heart to the ace.

Tricks 5-6: Cash the queen of spades and jack of spades.

Trick 7: Play a diamond to the king.

Tricks 8-9: Cash the king and queen of hearts. You have won the first nine tricks.

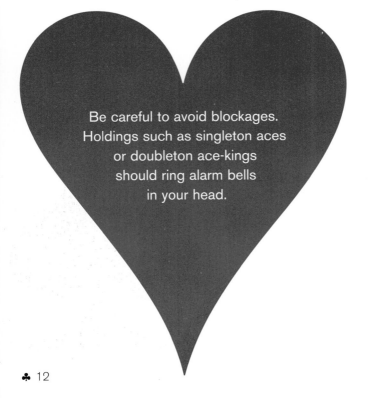

Be careful to avoid blockages. Holdings such as singleton aces or doubleton ace-kings should ring alarm bells in your head.

deal 3
mind that entry

```
              ♠ AK6
              ♥ KJ10
              ♦ A872
              ♣ 1062
  ♠ Q94      ┌─────────┐    ♠ J1075
  ♥ 97642    │    N    │    ♥ Q8
  ♦ K43      │ W     E │    ♦ QJ109
  ♣ 73       │    S    │    ♣ A95
              └─────────┘
              ♠ 832
              ♥ A53
              ♦ 65
              ♣ KQJ84
```

South	West	North	East
–	–	1♦	Pass
1NT	Pass	2NT	Pass
3NT	All Pass		

West leads the six of hearts against your
3NT. Plan the play.

How many winners do you have?

In top tricks you have: 2 in spades, 3 in hearts (after the lead, if you play the jack or ten of hearts from dummy you will make three tricks in the suit whoever has the queen) and 1 in diamonds = 6
In delayed tricks you have: 4 in clubs
In total you have 10 sure winners.

How many times will you need to lose the lead to establish your nine tricks?

Just once, when you knock out the ace of clubs.

What can go wrong?

There is no danger of the opponents establishing too many tricks, indeed the opening lead has done nothing to help their side establish any tricks at all.

Suppose you play the jack or ten of hearts from dummy at trick one in order to guarantee your three tricks in the suit. If West has led from the queen and your honor holds the trick, there is no problem, but what if East covers with the queen? If you win with the ace you have no entry to the club suit if the ace is held up until the third round.

When you counted your winners, you arrived at a total of ten, one more than you need. The solution is to give up that extra heart trick to guarantee making four in clubs.

The play

Trick 1:   Win the king of hearts.
Tricks 2-4:   Play clubs. East holds off until the third round.
Trick 5:   East switches to a diamond. Which you win with the ace.
Trick 6:   Play the jack of hearts. On this occasion East plays the queen. You win with the ace (which you would have done even had East played low).
Tricks 7-11:   Cash your remaining two clubs, your ace and king of spades and your ten of hearts for a total of ten tricks.

When you have counted your tricks, make sure that you do all that you can to preserve entries to the winners in your long suits.

deal 4
ducking your own lead

```
                    ♠  64
                    ♥  873
                    ♦  AK8732
                    ♣  94
    ♠  Q10752    ┌─────────┐    ♠  J98
    ♥  A964      │    N    │    ♥  K52
    ♦  Q5        │ W     E │    ♦  J106
    ♣  J7        │    S    │    ♣  Q1086
                 └─────────┘
                    ♠  AK3
                    ♥  QJ10
                    ♦  94
                    ♣  AK532
```

South	West	North	East
1NT	Pass	3NT	All Pass

West leads the five of spades against your 3NT.
Plan the play.

How many winners do you have?

In top tricks you have: 2 in spades, 2 in diamonds and 2 in clubs = 6
In delayed tricks you have: 1 in hearts
In total you have 7 sure winners.

For the first time there is a hand where you have insufficient sure winners and must look at 'possible tricks'. In this case a favorable distribution in a minor suit will provide the 'possible' tricks you need. If clubs break 3-3 you can establish two extra tricks there (36% chance), but there is a much better chance that diamonds break 3-2 (about 68%) and you can establish three extra winners in that suit.

There is an additional reason for choosing to play on diamonds. As well as offering the best chance, it will produce, if successful, three extra winners thus removing the need to establish a heart trick.

What can go wrong?

If you simply play out ace, king and another diamond you may establish three extra winners in the suit but you will not be able to reach them.

Is there a solution to this problem?

There are often advantages to losing the first round of a suit. If you start by playing a small diamond from both hands and the suit breaks 3-2 you will later be able to cash five diamonds.

The play

Trick 1: Win your king of spades.

Trick 2: Play the nine of diamonds from hand and the two from dummy whatever West plays (unless he shows out when you should change your mind and play on clubs instead). Say East wins with the ten.

Trick 3: Win the spade continuation with the ace.

Tricks 4-13: Cash five more diamonds followed by the ace and king of clubs for your contract. Nine tricks in all.

When you have to lose a trick in a suit it is often best to lose the first trick.

deal 5
delayed entry

```
                ♠  QJ6
                ♥  762
                ◆  QJ82
                ♣  854
    ♠  K10953  ┌─────────┐  ♠  72
    ♥  J8      │    N    │  ♥  Q1095
    ◆  106543  │  W   E  │  ◆  97
    ♣  7       │    S    │  ♣  KQJ102
                └─────────┘
                ♠  A84
                ♥  AK43
                ◆  AK
                ♣  A963
```

South	West	North	East
2NT	Pass	3NT	All Pass

West leads the ten of spades against your
3NT. Plan the play.

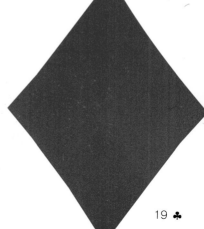

19 ♣

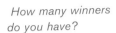

How many winners do you have?

In top tricks you have:
2 in spades (since West has led one), 2 in hearts, 4 in diamonds and 1 in clubs = 9
You have no delayed tricks
In total you have 9 sure winners.

What can go wrong?

Suppose you play the queen of spades from dummy at trick one. As it happens West has led away from his king and the queen holds the trick. Your diamond suit is blocked. You have four winners in the suit but after you have cashed your ace-king you have no way back to dummy for the queen-jack.

Is there a solution to this problem?

If you refuse to play one of dummy's spade honors at trick one, instead winning in hand with your ace, you cannot be prevented from reaching dummy with a spade honor later.

The play

Trick 1: Win West's ten of spades with your ace.

Tricks 2-3: Cash the ace and king of diamonds.

Trick 4: Play a spade. West wins with the king.

Trick 5: West continues with a third spade which you win in dummy with the queen.

Tricks 6-7: Cash the queen and jack of diamonds.

Tricks 8-13: You have six tricks stacked in front of you and you still have the ace and king of of hearts and the ace of clubs left. You concede the last three tricks to the opponents.

When one hand is quite weak, try to preserve as many entries to that hand as possible.

deal 6
losing an unnecessary trick

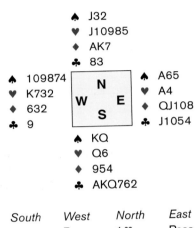

♠ J32
♥ J10985
♦ AK7
♣ 83

♠ 109874
♥ K732
♦ 632
♣ 9

♠ A65
♥ A4
♦ QJ108
♣ J1054

♠ KQ
♥ Q6
♦ 954
♣ AKQ762

South	West	North	East
1♣	Pass	1♥	Pass
3♣	Pass	3♦	Pass
3NT	All Pass		

West leads the ten of spades against your
3NT. East wins with the ace and returns the
six which you win in hand with the king.
Plan the play.

How many winners do you have?

In top tricks you have: 2 in spades (since the ace has been played), 2 in diamonds and 3 in clubs = 7
In delayed tricks you have: 3 in hearts
In total you have 10 sure winners.

How many times will you need to lose the lead to establish your nine tricks?

Twice to knock out both the ace and king of hearts.

What can go wrong?

East may win the first heart and clear the spades. Then West may get the lead with the other heart honor and cash his spades. The defenders would then have taken five tricks.

Is there a solution to this problem?

Sometimes, although you have sufficient sure tricks, you do not have the 'time' to make them and a different solution must be sought. Here, although you have only counted on making three club tricks, you have a tremendous trick-taking potential there. After all, if the suit breaks 3-2 (68% of the time) you will have six tricks, taking your overall total to ten.

Is there any other problem?

If you win the king of spades and play your clubs from the top you will be OK if they break 3-2 but if they break 4-1 you will have to lose a trick in the suit and you have no entry back to the South hand to cash your two established winners.

The solution is to give up one of your possible tricks in the suit voluntarily. Play a low club from both hands initially and now you will make five tricks (all you need for your contract) in the suit even if it breaks 4-1. This is called a 'safety play'.

The play

Trick 1: East wins the ace of spades.
Trick 2: Win East's spade continuation with your king.
Trick 3: Play the two of clubs. West's nine wins the trick.
Trick 4: Win the spade continuation with dummy's jack.
Tricks 5-13: Play the eight of clubs to your ace. Run the remaining four club tricks and cash the ace and king of diamonds for your contract.

Always be on the look-out for 'safety plays' – work out how many tricks you need from any given suit and then try to find the most secure way to make them.

make sure of those tricks

```
              ♠  A10984
              ♥  73
              ♦  AJ32
              ♣  92
♠  76          ┌─────────┐      ♠  J532
♥  A9652       │    N    │      ♥  J84
♦  K10         │  W   E  │      ♦  Q975
♣  Q1083       │    S    │      ♣  J6
              └─────────┘
              ♠  KQ
              ♥  KQ10
              ♦  864
              ♣  AK754
```

South	West	North	East
1NT	Pass	3♠	Pass
3NT	All Pass		

West leads the five of hearts against your
3NT. East plays the jack and you
win with your queen. Plan the
play.

deal 8
ducking the opening lead

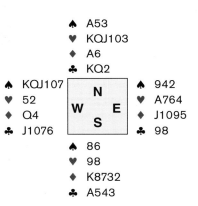

```
              ♠ A53
              ♥ KQJ103
              ♦ A6
              ♣ KQ2
♠ KQJ107                      ♠ 942
♥ 52          N              ♥ A764
♦ Q4        W   E            ♦ J1095
♣ J1076       S              ♣ 98
              ♠ 86
              ♥ 98
              ♦ K8732
              ♣ A543
```

South	West	North	East
–	–	1♥	Pass
1NT	Pass	3NT	All Pass

West leads the king of spades against your
3NT. Plan the play.

How many winners do you have?

In top tricks you have: 1 in spades, 2 in diamonds and 3 in clubs = 6
In delayed tricks you have: 4 in hearts
In total you have 10 sure winners.

How many times will you need to lose the lead to establish your tricks?

Just once, when you knock out the ace of hearts.

What can go wrong?

There are no problems with entries this time, North having many more than you need. However, if you win the ace of spades and play a heart there is a danger that the defenders will win the ace and cash four spade tricks, putting you one down.

Is there a solution to this problem?

If the opponents' spades break 4-4 there is no problem; all they can ever take is one heart and three spade tricks. However, if one opponent has five spades there is a problem. You can still make your contract provided he does not have the ace of hearts. You must 'duck' the king of spades, i.e. not win your ace this time. If you hold off your ace until the third round you will exhaust one opponent of the suit and if he is the one with the ace of hearts you will be home.

The play

Tricks 1-2: Play a low spade from both hands.

Trick 3: Win the ace of spades in dummy.

Trick 4: Play the king of hearts (East will probably win the ace and play a club, hoping his partner has the ace as an entry).

Tricks 5-13: Win East's club return with dummy's king, cash dummy's remaining four hearts, followed by the queen and ace of clubs and the ace and king of diamonds. Finally try the five of clubs. If the suit breaks 3-3 (or if an opponent has made a mistake and discarded one on a heart) you will make two overtricks. But always take the tricks you are certain of first.

When you have only the ace in the suit that the opponents have led it is usually right to hold off for a couple of rounds.

a double stopper

```
              ♠  Q53
              ♥  A10542
              ♦  94
              ♣  K62
♠  642                        ♠  10987
♥  Q9          N              ♥  K876
♦  K65      W     E           ♦  A72
♣  QJ984       S              ♣  107
              ♠  AKJ
              ♥  J3
              ♦  QJ1083
              ♣  A53
```

South	West	North	East
1NT	Pass	3♥	Pass
3NT	All Pass		

West leads the queen of clubs against your
3NT. Plan the play.

How many winners do you have?

In top tricks you have: 3 in spades, 1 in hearts and 2 in clubs = 6

In delayed tricks you have: 3 in diamonds

In total you have 9 sure winners.

How many times will you need to lose the lead to establish your nine tricks?

Twice, when you knock out the ace and king of diamonds.

What can go wrong?

If one opponent (probably West) has five clubs and both the ace and king of diamonds there is nothing you can do. You win the club and play a diamond, but he wins and clears the clubs. He will then get in with the other diamond honor to cash his clubs. If East has both diamond honors there is no problem. When you knock out the first diamond honor he will return a club to clear the suit but when he gets in with the second diamond he will not have a club to return (unless the suit breaks 4-3 when you can't go down anyway).

More often, the diamond honors will be split, with West and East having one each. If you win the first club and play a diamond, East will win his honor and clear clubs, leaving West with the other diamond honor as entry.

Is there a solution to this problem?

Duck the first club. Now when East wins his diamond honor he will have no club to return and the suit cannot be established.

The play

> Trick 1: Play a low club from both hands.
> Trick 2: West continues the suit and you win dummy's king of clubs
> Trick 3: Play the nine of diamonds. West wins the king and continue clubs.
> Trick 4: Win the ace of clubs.
> Trick 5: Play the queen of diamonds. East wins his ace and returns a spade.
> Tricks 6-13: Win the king of spades in hand, cash your remaining three diamonds, the other top spades and the ace of hearts for nine tricks.

If you have to lose the lead twice to set up your tricks, it may be right to duck the opening lead even with a double stopper.

deal 10
ducking gives up a trick

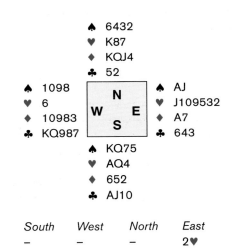

```
            ♠ 6432
            ♥ K87
            ♦ KQJ4
            ♣ 52
  ♠ 1098           ♠ AJ
  ♥ 6        N     ♥ J109532
  ♦ 10983  W   E   ♦ A7
  ♣ KQ987     S    ♣ 643
            ♠ KQ75
            ♥ AQ4
            ♦ 652
            ♣ AJ10
```

South	West	North	East
–	–	–	2♥
2NT	Pass	3NT	All Pass

West leads the king of clubs against your 3NT. East plays the three. Plan the play.

North/South did well in the bidding to avoid their 4-4 spade fit. West also did well not to lead his partner's suit, after which there would have been no problems.

How many tricks do you have?

In top tricks you have: 3 in hearts and 1 in clubs
= 4
In delayed tricks you have: 1 in spades and 2 in
diamonds = 3
In total you have 7 sure winners.

Where are the other two to come from?

If you win the ace of clubs and play the jack back
(now or later) you will make an extra trick with the
ten. There are other possibilities: if, as is nearly
certain from the bidding, East has the ace of
spades then the spade suit will generate at least
two tricks, three if the suit breaks 3-2 (about 68%
of the time); if diamonds break 3-3 there will be an
extra trick there.

Can you see any problems?

Yes, if East has three small
clubs. If you win the ace of
clubs and knock out an
ace he will continue
clubs. West will duck and
then when East gets in the
defenders will be able to
take three clubs. On the other
hand, if you duck the king of
clubs at trick one, although you
may give up a trick in the suit you
neutralise the West hand.

The play

Trick 1: Let West's king of clubs hold the trick.

Trick 2: West switches to the six of hearts. Note that it wouldn't help West to continue clubs as that would give you a second trick in the suit. You win in hand with the queen.

Trick 3: Play a diamond to dummy's king and East's ace.

Trick 4: East plays a second club. You duck and West wins with the queen.

Trick 5: West plays a third club which you win with the ace.

Trick 6: Play a diamond to the queen.

Trick 7: Play a spade to your queen.

Trick 8: Play a heart to the king.

Trick 9: Play a second spade. East wins the ace but has no club to play. Instead he plays a heart.

Tricks 10-13: All you have left is winners: two spades, a heart and a diamond, nine tricks in all.

Sometimes it is right to duck, even at the expense of a trick – it is your contract that matters not one trick.

deal 11
lead up to honors

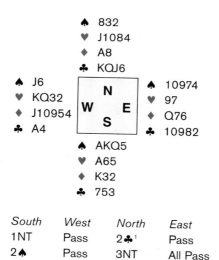

```
                ♠  832
                ♥  J1084
                ♦  A8
                ♣  KQJ6
♠  J6                        ♠  10974
♥  KQ32        N            ♥  97
♦  J10954   W     E         ♦  Q76
♣  A4          S            ♣  10982
                ♠  AKQ5
                ♥  A65
                ♦  K32
                ♣  753
```

South	West	North	East
1NT	Pass	2♣¹	Pass
2♠	Pass	3NT	All Pass

¹ a convention used to ask for four-card major suits in order to locate a 4-4 major-suit fit

West leads the jack of diamonds against your 3NT. Plan the play.

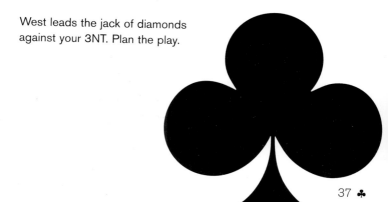

How many winners do you have?

In top tricks you have: 3 in spades, 1 in hearts and
2 in diamonds = 6
In delayed tricks you have: 2 in clubs
In total you have 8 sure winners.

Where is the ninth to come from?

There are two possibilities: spades or clubs
(although you could probably establish an extra
trick in hearts it would not be before the defenders
had established five tricks first). If spades break 3-3
there will be no problem. Your chances in clubs are
better: either a 3-3 break or the ace with West.

Can you see any problems?

The spade suit can
wait. The first
priority is to knock
out the ace of
clubs. If the suit
breaks 3-3 there
is no difficulty but
if it does not and
West has the ace
you must be careful to
lead up to dummy's
honor combination,
possibly as many as three
times. To do this you need to
use your entries carefully.

The play

Trick 1: Win the king of diamonds in your hand.

Trick 2: Play a club. West will probably play low and the jack will win.

Trick 3: Play a spade to your ace.

Trick 4: Play a second club. In this instance West will win with the ace and all your problems are over. However, if the second club held the trick you would need to play a spade to your king and play a third club.

Trick 5: West continues with a diamond on which dummy plays the ace and East the queen.

Tricks 6-10: Cash your remaining winners: two (or three) in spades, one in hearts and two in clubs.

Provided you have the entries it is usually best to lead up to honor combinations.

deal 12
the finesse

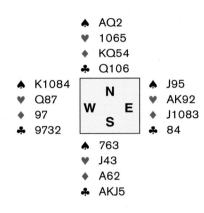

	♠	AQ2
	♥	1065
	♦	KQ54
	♣	Q106

♠ K1084		♠ J95
♥ Q87	N	♥ AK92
♦ 97	W E	♦ J1083
♣ 9732	S	♣ 84

	♠	763
	♥	J43
	♦	A62
	♣	AKJ5

South	West	North	East
1♣	Pass	1♦	Pass
1NT	Pass	3NT	All Pass

West leads the four of spades against your 3NT.
Plan the play.

In top tricks you have: 1 in spades, 3 in diamonds and 4 in clubs = 8
You have no delayed tricks.
In total you have 8 sure winners.

Where is the ninth to come from?

There are two possibilities.
Diamonds may break
3-3, giving you four tricks in the suit. The other possibility is that the queen of spades will make a trick.

In the Introduction we touched on the finesse. Suppose you have AQx of a suit in dummy and xxx in hand. If you play the ace and then a little one you will only ever make one trick in the suit (unless the king is singleton or doubleton). If you lead small from your hand, playing the queen whenever the next hand plays low, you will make two tricks whenever that player holds the king.

The position is the same when West has led the suit as he is quite likely to lead from a king against a no trump contract if that is his longest and strongest suit.

On a different lead you would have hoped to test the diamonds to see if they were 3-3 before taking

How many winners do you have?

In top tricks you have: 1 in spades, 1 in hearts, 1 in diamonds and 4 in clubs = 7

In delayed tricks you have: 1 (or more) in diamonds

In total you have 8 sure winners, just the right number.

Can you see any problems?

Suppose you win the ace of hearts and play a diamond to the ace and another diamond. East will win his king and the defenders will cash three heart tricks. They will then switch to spades, setting up two or three tricks in that suit before you have established a second diamond trick.

What is the solution?

Provided that West holds at least one of the king and queen of diamonds, you can make a second diamond trick while losing the lead only once. You first run the jack of diamonds to East's honor. When you regain the lead you run the ten of diamonds; West must either cover, setting up your nine, or duck when your ten will hold the trick.

Trick 1: Win the ace of hearts

Trick 2: Run the jack of diamonds to East's king.

Tricks 3-5: The defenders cash three heart tricks.

Trick 6: West switches to the five of spades. East plays the ten and you win with the ace.

Tricks 7-10: Cash your four club tricks ending in hand (after all if you *do* lose another diamond trick to East you may as well go only two down).

Trick 11: Play the ten of diamonds, running it if West plays low.

Trick 12: Cash the ace of diamonds, your eighth trick.

Even when you have to lose a trick in a suit, if you lose it in the right way you can give yourself a good chance of a successful finesse later on.

deal 14
another double finesse

```
            ♠  J64
            ♥  53
            ♦  762
            ♣  AQ1098
♠ 983                        ♠ 10752
♥ Q87          N             ♥ AK42
♦ J983      W     E          ♦ Q104
♣ K43          S             ♣ J5
            ♠  AKQ
            ♥  J1096
            ♦  AK5
            ♣  762
```

South	West	North	East
1NT	Pass	2NT	Pass
3NT	All Pass		

West leads the three of diamonds against your
3NT, East playing the
queen. Plan the play.

In top tricks you have: 3 in spades, 2 in diamonds and 1 in clubs = 6
In delayed tricks you have: 2 in clubs (if you play the ace and then the queen someone will win the king, later you play the ten and someone will win the jack, leaving you the nine and eight as winners; thus you have two extra 'delayed' tricks)
In total you have 8 sure winners.

Where is the ninth to come from?

It may be possible to establish a heart, but that would mean losing the lead three times in the suit and surely by then East/West would have set up two diamond tricks. The best chance is in the club suit.

The club suit on this hand is another example of a double finesse. First you lead a club towards dummy and play the ten (or the nine or the eight). If it holds the trick you come back to hand and play towards dummy again. It looks as if West has both the king and jack and you will make a total of five club tricks. It is more likely that the ten of clubs will lose to East's jack or king. In either event you later return to hand and take a second finesse in the suit. If East shows out it may be necessary to come to hand yet again and take a third finesse.

What can go wrong?

There is nothing further to consider in this instance. You have plenty of entries to hand. Either the club suit will generate the required number of tricks or it won't.

The play

Trick 1: Win the king of diamonds.

Trick 2: Play a club to the ten which, as it happens, loses to East's jack.

Trick 3: Win the diamond return with the ace.

Trick 4: Play another club. West plays low and you play the queen which holds the trick, East following small.

Tricks 5-13: Cash three more club tricks and three top spades for your contract.

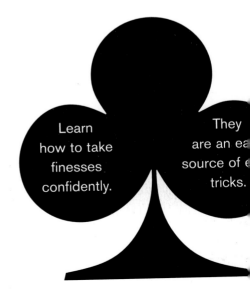

Learn how to take finesses confidently.

They are an ea source of e tricks.

deal 15
more finessing

```
              ♠ J42
              ♥ K8743
              ♦ 732
              ♣ A2
♠ K5                          ♠ Q987
♥ Q105        N              ♥ J96
♦ K6       W     E           ♦ Q104
♣ J109764     S              ♣ 853
              ♠ A1063
              ♥ A2
              ♦ AJ985
              ♣ KQ
```

South	West	North	East
1 ♦	Pass	1 ♥	Pass
1 ♠	Pass	2 ♦	Pass
2NT	Pass	3NT	All Pass

West leads the jack of clubs against your 3NT.
Plan the play.

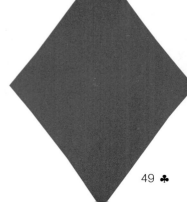

49 ♣

How many winners do you have?

In top tricks you have: 1 in spades, 2 in hearts, 1 in diamonds and 2 in clubs = 6
You have no delayed tricks
In total you have 6 sure winners.

Where are the extra three to come from?

There are several possibilities:

1) Hearts: if the suit breaks 3-3 you can establish two extra tricks there, bringing your total to eight.

2) Spades: if the suit breaks 3-3 and East holds both the king and the queen you can establish two extra tricks there, bringing your total to eight.

3) Diamonds: if the king and queen are divided between East and West with East holding the ten, you can establish three extra tricks in the suit, bringing your total to nine.

Clearly (3) is most attractive, simply because it offers the possibility of that vital, contract-fulfilling trick. In addition, it happens to offer the best chance, roughly 37%.

How many times will you need to lose the lead to establish your nine tricks?

Hopefully just once, to either the king or queen of diamonds.

What can go wrong?

It is best to win the first trick in the dummy in order to play a diamond immediately. You then have a further entry in the king of hearts to play diamonds again.

The play

Trick 1: Win the ace of clubs.

Trick 2: Play a diamond to the eight which, as it happens, loses to West's king.

Trick 3: Win the club return with the king.

Trick 4: Play a heart to the king (cashing the ace first achieves nothing and will lead to more down if West has the queen of diamonds).

Trick 5: Play a diamond. East plays the ten, you play the jack and it holds the trick.

Tricks 6-13: Cash two more diamonds, the ace of hearts and ace of spades to make your contract.

Sometimes finesses help you to reduce your number of losers in a suit, even if they do not eliminate them altogether.

deal 16
find the lady

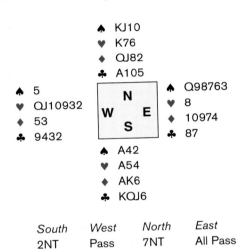

```
                    ♠ KJ10
                    ♥ K76
                    ♦ QJ82
                    ♣ A105
    ♠ 5                          ♠ Q98763
    ♥ QJ10932      N             ♥ 8
    ♦ 53        W     E          ♦ 10974
    ♣ 9432         S             ♣ 87
                    ♠ A42
                    ♥ A54
                    ♦ AK6
                    ♣ KQJ6
```

South	West	North	East
South	*West*	*North*	*East*
2NT	Pass	7NT	All Pass

West leads the queen of hearts against your 7NT.
When dummy comes down you see that your
partner has been a little overenthusiastic. You
have shown 21-22 points, so he really
should have in the region of 16 before
jumping to 7NT. Still, it is not a bad
contract. Plan the play.

In top tricks you have: 2 in spades,
2 in hearts, 4 in diamonds and 4 in
clubs = 12
You have no delayed tricks (not
much use in a grand slam in any
event!)
In total you have 12 sure winners.

Where is the thirteenth to come from?

The only possibility is spades. You will have to
guess who has the queen. Well, you could do
this straight away but it would be much better
to try to find out about the opponents' distribution.

The plan is to cash all your winners outside
spades. If you can find out which hand has the
longer spades the odds would favour playing that
hand for the queen.

The play

Trick 1: Win the ace of hearts.
Tricks 2-5: Cash four club tricks. West follows
suit while East discards two spades.
You throw a heart from dummy.
Tricks 6-9: Cash four diamond tricks. East follows
suit and West discards two hearts.
You throw a heart from hand.
Trick 10: Cash dummy's king of hearts. East
discards a spade.

Everyone now has three cards left. Dummy has KJ10 of spades and you have A42. You need to pause to work out what you know about the hand. East had only two clubs, he had four diamonds and he had one heart. Therefore he started with six spades and West with a singleton. The contract is now certain.

Trick 11: Cash dummy's king of spades.
Tricks 12-13: Lead the jack of spades, playing low from hand when East follows small. West discards a heart and you claim the last trick.

This deal turned out very luckily because you were able to get a total count of the hand so that in the end there was no guess at all. This is not usually the case. If you can find out which opponent has greater length in the suit (or has fewer cards in the other suits) then that opponent is more likely to have any missing honor. Usually your careful counting will merely improve your chances rather than make your chosen play a sure thing.

Try to leave critical decision until you have as much information as possible.

deal 17
an incomplete picture

```
              ♠  KQ105
              ♥  K76
              ♦  7632
              ♣  Q6
♠  J984            N        ♠  62
♥  Q1082      W       E     ♥  J94
♦  J               S        ♦  10985
♣  A1073                    ♣  K985
              ♠  A73
              ♥  A53
              ♦  AKQ4
              ♣  J42
```

South	West	North	East
1NT	Pass	2♣¹	Pass
2♦	Pass	3NT	All Pass

¹ Stayman

West leads the two of hearts
against your 3NT. Plan the play.

How many winners do you have?

In top tricks you have: 3 in spades, 2 in
hearts and 3 in diamonds = 8
You have no delayed tricks
In total you have 8 sure winners.

Where is the ninth to come from?

There are three possibilities. If
diamonds break 3-2 there are nine
tricks on top. The ninth trick could also
come from a spade break or a successful
finesse of the ten on the *third* round (playing West
to have started with Jxxx). It is just possible
that clubs could provide the ninth trick but
this type of combination is much more
useful if the opponents play the suit.

The play

Trick 1: Win the ace of hearts.
Trick 2: Cash the ace of diamonds. It is best
to play diamonds before spades
because you have no choice on how
you play the diamond suit. In
spades, on the other hand, you
could play for a 3-3 break or for
West to have Jxxx in the suit, so
leave that suit until you know more
about the hand.
Trick 3: Cash the king of diamonds. West
discards a club.

You now know that West started with four hearts and one diamond. It is unlikely that he started with five clubs or he would surely have preferred to lead that suit at trick one. If he has at most four clubs then he has at least four spades.

Trick 4: Play a spade to dummy's king.

Trick 5: Play a spade back to your ace. Notice that if East had the jack it would have appeared by now.

Trick 7: Play a spade to dummy's ten. On this occasion East discards a club.

Tricks 8-13: Cash your queen of spades, queen of diamonds and king of hearts, nine tricks in total.

It is usually safe to assume that a defender will not have a longer unbid suit than the one he leads at trick one. This inference can help you to count a hand.

deal 18
where are the majors?

```
               ♠  873
               ♥  954
               ♦  A85
               ♣  KJ109
  ♠ Q105     ┌─────────┐     ♠ J942
  ♥ KJ2      │    N    │     ♥ Q10876
  ♦ Q1074    │  W   E  │     ♦ J9
  ♣ Q53      │    S    │     ♣ 62
             └─────────┘
               ♠  AK6
               ♥  A3
               ♦  K632
               ♣  A874
```

South	West	North	East
1NT	Pass	2NT	Pass
3NT	All Pass		

West leads the four of diamonds against your 3NT. Plan the play.

How many winners do you have?

In top tricks you have: 2 in spades, 1 in hearts, 2 in diamonds and 2 in clubs = 7
In delayed tricks you have: 1 in clubs
In total you have 8 sure winners.

Where is the extra trick to come from?

After the diamond lead it is very unlikely that that suit will break 3-3. So your only chance is to make four club tricks.

What is the best way to play the club suit?

Superficially, the finesse is a 50% shot. You can pick up the queen in either hand, even if the suit breaks 5-0. You simply have to guess who has it. The defender with the most cards in a given suit is more likely to have any particular cards in that suit. If you knew which defender that was you would play him for the queen. The clue is in the opening lead. You bid to 3NT without using Stayman to look for a 4-4 major-suit fit. Put yourself in West's position. You know he has led a four-card diamond suit (the four is the lowest outstanding spot card). Wouldn't you prefer a four-card major to a scrappy four-card diamond suit? West is very likely to have 3-3-4-3 or 3-2-4-4 distribution, so you should play him for the queen.

The play

Trick 1: Win the king of diamonds.

Trick 2: Cash the ace of clubs.

Trick 3: Play a club. When West plays low play the ten from dummy. In this instance it holds the trick, East following small.

Tricks 4-9: Cash two more clubs, one more diamond, one heart and two spades, nine tricks in all.

The player with the greater length in a suit is likely to hold any missing honor card in that suit. The opening lead can often give you a clue as to the distribution of the hand.

deal 19
counting points

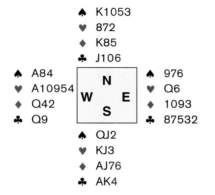

♠ K1053
♥ 872
♦ K85
♣ J106

♠ A84
♥ A10954
♦ Q42
♣ Q9

N
W E
S

♠ 976
♥ Q6
♦ 1093
♣ 87532

♠ QJ2
♥ KJ3
♦ AJ76
♣ AK4

South	West	North	East
–	1 ♥	Pass	Pass
2NT	Pass	3NT	All Pass

West leads the five of hearts against your 3NT.
East plays the queen. Plan the play.

In top tricks you have: 1 in hearts (after the lead), 2 in diamonds and 2 in clubs = 5

In delayed tricks you have: 3 in spades

In total you have 8 sure winners.

Where is the ninth to come from?

There are two main possibilities. Diamonds and clubs. Or perhaps West may be persuaded to lead another heart − although that sort of thing may well happen at the table, it seldom does in bridge books!

What is the danger?

West is marked with all the outstanding points so taking a minor-suit finesse into his hand is bound to lose. East gaining the lead to push a heart through your vulnerable holding could be a danger but you know he has no high card left.

The play

> Trick 1: Win the king of hearts.
> Trick 2: Play the queen of spades. West wins with the ace.
> Trick 3: Win West's spade return with the jack.
> Trick 4: Cash the king of spades.
> Trick 5: Cash the ten of spades. East discards a club, you a diamond and West a heart.

It looks as if West started with three spades and five hearts. One of his minor-suit queens must be doubleton.

> Trick 6: Cash the king of diamonds.
> Trick 7: Play a diamond to your ace.
> Trick 8: Cash the ace of clubs.
> Trick 9: Cash the king of clubs and watch West's queen come tumbling down.

When an opponent has opened the bidding you can assume he has at least 12 points which may well help you place the high cards.

deal 20
but he never bid...

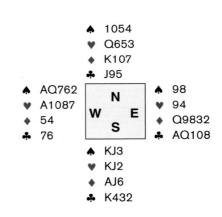

```
              ♠ 1054
              ♥ Q653
              ♦ K107
              ♣ J95
  ♠ AQ762              ♠ 98
  ♥ A1087      N       ♥ 94
  ♦ 54      W     E    ♦ Q9832
  ♣ 76         S       ♣ AQ108
              ♠ KJ3
              ♥ KJ2
              ♦ AJ6
              ♣ K432
```

South	West	North	East
–	Pass	Pass	Pass
1NT	All Pass		

West leads the six of spades against your 1NT.
East plays the nine. Plan the play.

How many winners do you have?

In top tricks you have: 1 in spades (after the lead) and 2 in diamonds = 3
In delayed tricks you have: 2 in hearts
In total you have 5 sure winners.

Where are the others to come from?

There are three possibilities, two of which need to work for you: a 3-3 heart break, a successful diamond finesse or the king of clubs may make a trick. The first thing to do is set about establishing your delayed tricks.

The play

Trick 1: Win the jack of spades.
Trick 2: Play a heart to the queen.
Trick 3: Play a heart to the king. West wins the ace.
Trick 4: West plays the seven of clubs to East's ace. You now have six top tricks.
Trick 5: East plays a spade and your king loses to West's ace.
Tricks 6-8: West cashes three spade tricks. East discards two diamonds and a club. Dummy discards clubs. You discard two clubs. You have now lost six tricks.

You know that West cannot have the queen of diamonds. He passed as dealer and has shown up with a five-card spade suit and ten points already (the ace and queen of spades and the ace of hearts).

Trick 9: West plays a club. You discard a diamond from dummy. East plays the ten and you win the king.

Trick 10: Cash the jack of hearts. East discards a club.

Trick 11: Play a diamond to dummy's king.

Tricks 12-13: Play a diamond to your jack and claim the last trick when it holds.

When an opponent has passed as dealer you know he has at most 11 points (12 if he doesn't have a five-card suit).

deal 21
what strength no trump?

```
              ♠  A107
              ♥  1042
              ♦  AJ3
              ♣  QJ53
♠  985                        ♠  Q42
♥  AQJ6       N               ♥  853
♦  K108    W     E            ♦  9752
♣  A92        S               ♣  876
              ♠  KJ63
              ♥  K97
              ♦  Q64
              ♣  K104
```

South	West	North	East
–	1♣	Pass	Pass
1NT¹	Pass	3NT	All Pass

¹ While an overcall of 1NT directly over the
bidder would show 16-18 points, in fourth
seat it is normal to play it as showing about
11-15 points. The basic difference is
that East could not drum up a
response to the opening so he is
known to have a weak hand.

West leads the queen of hearts
against your 3NT. You win with the
king. Plan the play.

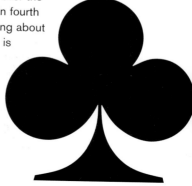

How many winners do you have?

In top tricks you have: 2 in spades, 1 in hearts (after the lead) and 1 in diamonds = 4
In delayed tricks you have: 1 in spades, 3 in clubs and 1 in diamonds = 5
In total you have 9 sure winners.

Can you see any problems?

When you lose your ace of clubs, West will no doubt cash some heart winners. However, it is very unlikely he has a five-card heart suit for his one club opening so you will have only three losers there to go with the ace of clubs. You can't afford any more losers. West is odds on to hold the king of diamonds so a finesse in that suit will bring your total up to eight. You will need to guess who has the queen of spades.

What is the best way to play the spade suit?

You know West has 7 high-card points in hearts, 3 in diamonds and 4 in clubs, 14 in all. He has a balanced hand but has not opened 1NT. If they play a strong no trump (16-18 points) he cannot have the queen of spades, otherwise he would have opened 1NT. Of course, if they played a weak no trump (12-14 points) you would know to play West for that card.

The play

Trick 1: Win the queen of hearts with the king.

Trick 2: Play the king of clubs. West wins with the ace.

Tricks 3-5: West cashes three heart tricks. On the third you discard a diamond from dummy and a spade from hand.

Trick 6: West gets off play with a club which you win in hand.

Trick 7: Play a diamond. When West plays low dummy's jack wins.

Tricks 8-9: Cash two clubs.

Trick 10: Cash the ace of spades.

Trick 11: Play a second spade. When East plays low, try the jack (these opponents play a strong 1NT, just like you).

Tricks 12-13: Cash the king of spades and the ace of diamonds.

If an opponent opens with one of a suit, the one thing he won't have is a balanced hand in his no trump range.

deal 22
a question of time

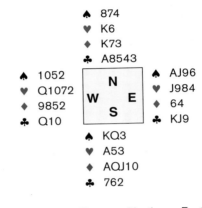

```
              ♠ 874
              ♥ K6
              ♦ K73
              ♣ A8543
♠ 1052                      ♠ AJ96
♥ Q1072      N              ♥ J984
♦ 9852    W     E           ♦ 64
♣ Q10        S              ♣ KJ9
              ♠ KQ3
              ♥ A53
              ♦ AQJ10
              ♣ 762
```

South	West	North	East
1NT	Pass	3NT	All Pass

West leads the two of hearts against
your 3NT. Plan the play.

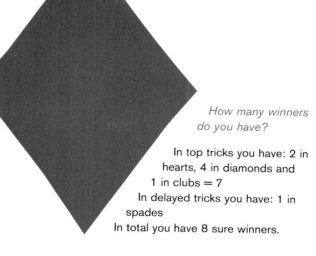

How many winners do you have?

In top tricks you have: 2 in hearts, 4 in diamonds and 1 in clubs = 7
In delayed tricks you have: 1 in spades
In total you have 8 sure winners.

Where is the ninth to come from?

There are two possibilities. There are good chances of developing two extra tricks in clubs. This would work any time the suit breaks 3-2. Then you would not need the delayed spade trick. This is roughly a 68% chance.

The alternative is to play for a second spade trick. Every time East has the ace of spades you can generate an extra trick in the suit simply by leading twice towards your hand. This is roughly a 50% chance.

It looks as though you should play on clubs.

How many times will you need to lose the lead before you establish nine tricks?

Twice. Ah, that is the problem. You win the heart lead. Play the ace of clubs and another club. They clear the hearts and can get in to cash them when they are in with the second club. And there is the

ace of spades. They will make five tricks: one
spade, two hearts and two clubs.

No, playing on clubs will see the opponents with
five tricks before you have nine. Better to take the
50% chance of the spade suit.

The play

Trick 1: Win the king of hearts.
Trick 2: Play a spade to your queen.
Trick 3: Play a diamond to the king.
Trick 4: Play a spade to your king, which
holds.
Tricks 5-13: Cash your top diamonds, ace of
hearts and ace of clubs, making nine
tricks in all.

You do not always have time to
establish your longest suit.
Sometimes you need to take a
lesser chance in another
suit in order to win the
race for tricks.

deal 23
a sure thing

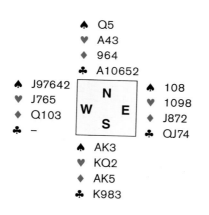

```
            ♠ Q5
            ♥ A43
            ♦ 964
            ♣ A10652
♠ J97642                    ♠ 108
♥ J765      N               ♥ 1098
♦ Q103    W   E             ♦ J872
♣ –         S               ♣ QJ74
            ♠ AK3
            ♥ KQ2
            ♦ AK5
            ♣ K983
```

South	West	North	East
2NT	Pass	4NT[1]	Pass
6NT	All Pass		

[1] inviting South to bid 6NT if he is maximum

West leads the six of spades against your 6NT. Plan the play.

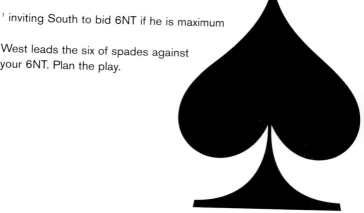

Slams are very exciting, both to bid and to play. However, beginners are often nervous about playing such high-level contracts. In many ways slams are quite easy to play as there are fewer alternatives. In any event, the thought processes are the same as for any other contract.

How many winners do you have?

In top tricks you have: 3 in spades, 3 in hearts, 2 in diamonds and 2 in clubs = 10 You have 1 or 2 delayed tricks in clubs.
In total you have 10 sure winners.

Where are the extra two to come from?

There is only one possibility, clubs. It should be possible to establish at least two extra tricks in that suit.

What can go wrong?

The only problem would be if one defender has all four missing clubs. You are lucky that there is a sure fire way to guard against that. Don't commit your ace or your king to the first trick in the suit, instead play a low club from one hand or the other and simply cover whatever card the next hand plays. Should he show out then you rise with the ace or king and play through the other hand.

The play

Trick 1: Win the queen of spades.
Trick 2: Play the two of clubs. When East plays the four, play the eight from your hand. West shows out, but it doesn't matter, you still have only one loser and four tricks in the suit.
Tricks 3-4: Cash the king and ace of clubs.
Trick 5: Concede a club to East.
Tricks 6-13: Claim all the rest of tricks whatever East plays.

Note that you could just as easily have won the king of spades in the South hand and played the three of clubs. When West showed out you would have risen with dummy's ace and played the two back, covering East's card.

Consider how to play different suit combinations. There is quite often a 100% way to play a suit for a given number of tricks.

deal 24
safety first

```
              ♠ KQJ4
              ♥ K5
              ♦ 42
              ♣ K7653
  ♠ 765                      ♠ 932
  ♥ J10942    N              ♥ Q873
  ♦ 8       W   E            ♦ J9763
  ♣ Q1082     S              ♣ J
              ♠ A108
              ♥ A6
              ♦ AKQ105
              ♣ A94
```

South	West	North	East
2NT	Pass	3♣¹	Pass
3♦	Pass	4♣	Pass
4♦	Pass	6NT	All Pass

¹ Stayman

West leads the jack of
hearts against your 6NT.
Plan the play.

How many winners do you have?

In top tricks you have: 4 in spades, 2 in
hearts, 3 in diamonds and 2 in clubs = 11
You have no delayed tricks.
In total you have 11 sure winners.

*Where is the twelfth trick to come
from?*

The best chance is in
diamonds but clubs offer
good prospects as
well.

Can you see any problems?

If diamonds are 4-2 or 3-3
everything will be easy. If they are
5-1 you can always change tack and
give up a club, hoping they break 3-2.

Can you see a way to improve on this plan?

If East is the one with five (or six) diamonds you
can still succeed. Start by cashing the ace of
diamonds, then cross to dummy and play a
second round of the suit. If East shows out, win
with the king and play on clubs. But if East
follows, just play the ten. If it holds you have the
four diamond tricks you need; if it loses the suit
must break 4-2 (or 3-3) and you also have four
tricks. This is another example of safety play.

Trick 1: Win the ace of hearts.

Trick 2: Cash the ace of diamonds.

Trick 3: Play a spade to the king.

Trick 4: Play a diamond. When East plays the six, play the ten from hand.

Tricks 5-12: Cash two more diamonds, three more spades, one more heart and two clubs, twelve in total. It is as well to leave clubs to the end as the defenders may go wrong, discarding a club too many to give you an overtrick.

When you are in a good contract, don't forget to look for a way to make it safer.

deal 25
when not to finesse

```
              ♠  AJ53
              ♥  A75
              ♦  104
              ♣  QJ64
   ♠ 9872        ┌─────────┐      ♠  Q10
   ♥ QJ1063      │    N    │      ♥  94
   ♦ K6          │ W     E │      ♦  AQ853
   ♣ 82          │    S    │      ♣  10953
                 └─────────┘
              ♠  K64
              ♥  K82
              ♦  J972
              ♣  AK7
```

South	West	North	East
1♦	Pass	1♠	Pass
1NT	Pass	3NT	All Pass

West leads the queen of hearts against
your 3NT. Plan the play.

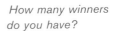

In top tricks you have: 2 in spades, 2 in hearts and 4 in clubs = 8
You have no delayed tricks
In total you have 8 sure winners.

Where is the ninth to come from?

There is only one real possibility, spades. The most likely chance is to find West with the queen of spades or the suit breaking 3-3. You have learned about finessing, so it could be right to cash the king of spades and then play low to the jack.

What can go wrong?

The trouble is that you don't want to lose a trick when East has the queen doubleton. You only need three spade tricks, not four, and you can afford to lose a trick in the suit. If you cash the ace, then the king and lead towards the jack you will make an extra trick whenever the suit is 3-3, or when West has the queen, or when East has queen doubleton. Note that it is important to play the *ace* of spades before the king or you will end up in the wrong hand.

The play

Trick 1: Win the king of hearts.

Trick 2: Play a spade to the ace.

Trick 3: Play a spade to the king. In the event East plays the queen and all your problems are over. Had he not done so you would have continued with a third spade towards the dummy, making the extra trick whenever West had the queen or the suit was 3-3

Tricks 4-13: Cash your clubs, your jack of spades and your ace of hearts, nine tricks in all.

Always work out how many tricks you need in any suit. Sometimes you don't need to finesse.

deal 26
how many tricks?

```
              ♠ A1073
              ♥ 106
              ♦ 8732
              ♣ K53
♠ Q64                        ♠ K985
♥ J873      ┌─────────┐      ♥ K954
♦ K         │    N    │      ♦ J65
♣ QJ1076    │  W   E  │      ♣ 98
            │    S    │
            └─────────┘
              ♠ J2
              ♥ AQ2
              ♦ AQ1094
              ♣ A42
```

South	West	North	East
1NT	Pass	2♣¹	Pass
2♦	Pass	2NT	Pass
3NT	All Pass		

¹ Stayman

West leads the queen of clubs against
your 3NT. Plan the play.

How many winners do you have?

In top tricks you have: 1 in spades, 1 in
hearts, 1 in diamonds and 2 in clubs = 5
In delayed tricks you have: 2 in diamonds
In total you have 7 sure winners.

Where are the other two to come from?

Hearts is a possibility for one trick, if East has
the king. Diamonds is the other hope as it is quite
likely that that suit will play for four or five winners.

What can go wrong?

If you take a straightforward diamond finesse,
playing to the queen, and it loses to the king
West will clear the clubs. Now what? If you cash
the queen of diamonds West may show out and
you will need to lose a trick to East's jack; if you
play a diamond to your ten West might win with
the jack and cash his clubs. No, the best play for
four diamond tricks if to start by cashing the ace.
An honor may drop and if it doesn't you can
continue by crossing to dummy and leading a
diamond towards your queen.

If you need five diamond tricks it is much better to
play small to your queen on the first round.

Here you don't know whether you need four or five
diamond tricks because you don't know how many
heart tricks you have.

How should you play the diamond suit?

The answer is that you must take the heart finesse first. If it loses West will clear the clubs and now you play a diamond to the queen, hoping for five diamond tricks. If the heart finesse holds, start by cashing the ace of diamonds, simply aiming for four tricks in the suit.

The play

Trick 1: Win the king of clubs.

Trick 2: Play a heart to your queen. On this occasion it holds the trick.

Trick 3: Cash the ace of diamonds. On this occasion West's king falls.

Trick 4: Play a spade to the ace.

Trick 5: Play a diamond to your ten. West shows out.

Tricks 6-13: Cash the three remaining diamond tricks, ace of hearts and ace of clubs for an overtrick.

Sometimes there is preparatory work to be done before you know how many tricks you need in a suit.

deal 27

keeping the right hand on lead

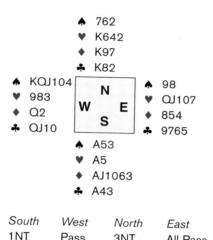

	♠ 762	
	♥ K642	
	♦ K97	
	♣ K82	
♠ KQJ104		♠ 98
♥ 983		♥ QJ107
♦ Q2		♦ 854
♣ QJ10		♣ 9765
	♠ A53	
	♥ A5	
	♦ AJ1063	
	♣ A43	

South	West	North	East
1NT	Pass	3NT	All Pass

West leads the king of spades against your 3NT.
You hold off until the third round, East
following twice and discarding a club
on the third spade. Plan the play.

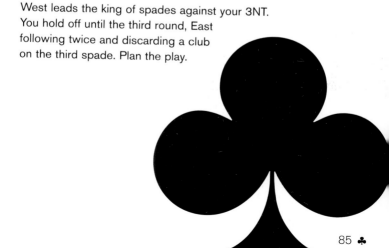

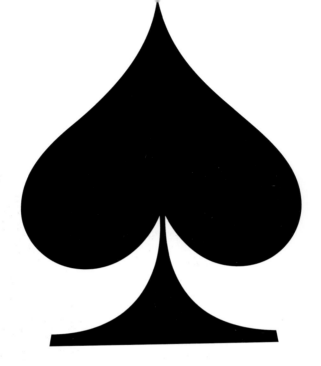

How many winners do you have?

In top tricks you have: 1 in spades, 2 in hearts, 2 in diamonds and 2 in clubs = 7
In delayed tricks you have: 2 in diamonds
In total you have 9 sure winners.

What can go wrong?

You need to make sure that West does not get the lead and cash his established spades. The normal way to play the diamond suit would be to cash the king and then lead towards your jack. Not a good idea on this occasion as West will cash his spades. On the other hand, if East wins a diamond he cannot harm you, so finesse into his hand.

The play

Tricks 1-2: Duck the first two spades.
Trick 3: Win the ace of spades.
Trick 4: Play the jack of diamonds, running it if West plays low. This time West plays the queen and you win dummy's king.
Tricks 5-8: Cash four more diamond tricks.
Tricks 9-13: Cash your ace and king of clubs and king of hearts. Ten tricks in all. The opponents will make the last trick.

Often there is one opponent to whom you would much prefer to lose the lead than another. If that is the case then you should try to take your finesses into his hand.

deal 28
more on avoidance

```
                    ♠ A87
                    ♥ 1062
                    ♦ AJ1032
                    ♣ J3
   ♠ Q1032      ┌──────────┐     ♠ J94
   ♥ K73        │    N     │     ♥ Q9854
   ♦ 76         │  W   E   │     ♦ K8
   ♣ K974       │    S     │     ♣ 865
               └──────────┘
                    ♠ K65
                    ♥ AJ
                    ♦ Q954
                    ♣ AQ102
```

South	West	North	East
1NT	Pass	3NT	All Pass

West leads the two of spades against your
3NT. Plan the play.

♣ 88

How many winners do you have?

In top tricks you have: 2 in spades,
1 in hearts, 1 in diamonds and
1 in clubs = 5
In delayed tricks you have:
3 in diamonds and 2 in clubs
= 5
In total you have 10 sure
winners.

What can go wrong?

The spade lead does not appear
to be much of a threat because
the two, if fourth highest, marks
West with a four-card suit only.

The danger suit is hearts but it is only a
problem if it is first played by East.
Suppose West gains the lead and
switches to a heart. East's queen will
force your ace but you will still have the jack and ten
to protect you against West's king. If, on the other
hand, East first plays the suit, you will play the jack
and West the king. West will return his seven and
you will have to play your ace whatever East plays
and the suit will be established for the opponents.

If both minor-suit kings are wrong you will need to
lose to both of them in order to arrive at nine tricks
and it is important that you first lose a trick to
West, who cannot attack hearts to advantage.

The play

Trick 1: Win the ace of spades.

Trick 2: Play the jack of clubs, losing on this layout to West.

Trick 3: Win West's spade continuation with the king. (It would not help him to switch to a heart.)

Trick 4: Play the ten of diamonds, losing to East's king.

Tricks 5-13: The defenders cannot harm you. If East plays a heart you win with the ace and make an overtrick (2 spades, 1 heart, 4 diamonds and 3 clubs). The best they can do is cash their spades and hold you to nine tricks.

When a trick must be lost to both opponents, consider which one to lose to first.

deal 29
when not to duck

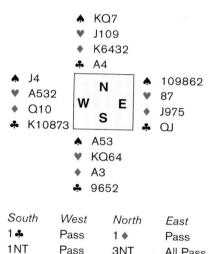

	♠ KQ7	
	♥ J109	
	♦ K6432	
	♣ A4	

♠ J4		♠ 109862
♥ A532	N	♥ 87
♦ Q10	W E	♦ J975
♣ K10873	S	♣ QJ

	♠ A53	
	♥ KQ64	
	♦ A3	
	♣ 9652	

South	West	North	East
1♣	Pass	1♦	Pass
1NT	Pass	3NT	All Pass

West leads the seven of clubs against your 3NT.
Plan the play.

How many winners do you have?

In top tricks you have: 3 in spades,
2 in diamonds and 1 in clubs = 6
In delayed tricks you have: 3 in hearts
In total you have 9 sure winners.

How many times will you need to lose the lead to establish your nine tricks?

Once when you knock out the ace of hearts.

What can go wrong?

If clubs are 4-3 there is no problem but what if they are 5-2? If East has the ace of hearts it would be right to duck the first club, but this will not help if West has the ace.

What can be done?

West has led the seven of clubs. There is a useful little mathematical formula that applies when playing fourth highest leads. It is called the 'Rule of Eleven'. You subtract the spot value of the card led (7) from 11 to arrive at the number (4) of cards higher than the seven in the other three hands. (It is easy to check this: there are 7 cards in total higher than the seven and West is known to have 3 of them, leaving 4 for the other three hands.) So there are four cards in the North, East and South hands that are higher than the seven and you can see two of them (the ace and the nine), leaving two for East. Surely if West had three of the four outstanding club honors he would have led one, therefore East must have two of them. If clubs are 4-3 it does not matter what you do but if they are 5-2 you can 'block' the suit by rising with dummy's ace at trick one.

The play

Trick 1: Win dummy's ace of clubs. East plays the queen.

Trick 2: Play a heart. West wins with the ace.

Trick 3: West plays a low club to his partner's jack but East is now out of the suit. It would not have helped West to play clubs from the top as this would have established your nine.

Tricks 4-13: East switches to a spade. You win in dummy with the queen, cash your heart winners followed by the king and ace of spades and ace and king of diamonds, nine tricks in total.

The 'Rule of Eleven' can help you work out how to block the opponents' suit.

deal 30
morton's fork

```
              ♠  A
              ♥  AK3
              ♦  KJ853
              ♣  QJ98
♠  QJ10964   ┌──────────┐    ♠  72
♥  J102      │    N     │    ♥  8764
♦  A6        │  W   E   │    ♦  10974
♣  A4        │    S     │    ♣  632
             └──────────┘
              ♠  K853
              ♥  Q95
              ♦  Q2
              ♣  K1075
```

South	West	North	East
–	1♠	Double	Pass
1NT	Pass	3NT	All Pass

West leads the queen of spades against your 3NT.
Plan the play.

♣ 94

How many winners do you have?

In top tricks you have: 2 in spades and 3 in
hearts = 5
In delayed tricks you have: 2 (or more)
in diamonds and 3 in clubs = 5
In total you have ten sure winners,
one more than you need.

Can you see any problems?

Suppose you win the ace of spades
and play a diamond to your queen.
West will win and knock out your second
spade stopper. If diamonds fail to break you will
need to make some club tricks but as soon as
West wins the ace of clubs he will win lots
of spades.

What is the solution?

You know that West has both minor-suit aces for
his opening bid. Look at the effect of coming to
hand with the queen of hearts and leading a *low*
diamond. If West goes in with his ace you make
four diamond tricks; if West ducks you change tack
and knock out the ace of clubs, making one
diamond and three club tricks.

The play

> Trick 1: Win the ace of spades.
> Trick 2: Play a heart to your queen.

Trick 3: Play a low diamond. In this instance West plays low and your jack wins in dummy.

Trick 4: Play the queen of clubs. West wins with the ace and continues spades.

Tricks 5-10: Win the king of spades and cash five more winners, two in hearts and three in clubs, bringing your total to nine.

This play of a low card towards an honor, presenting an opponent with a no-win situation where winning gives away an extra trick in the suit, but ducking allows you to turn your attention elsewhere, is known as Morton's Fork. It is named after Cardinal Morton, Chancellor under Henry VII, whose job was to extract revenue from London merchants. He took the view that if they lived lavishly they could obviously afford to pay the taxes; alternatively if they lived frugally they had obviously saved enough also to be able to afford to pay.

If you lead up to your honor combinations you may give an opponent no winning play: if he wins he presents you with an extra trick; if he ducks you move on to a different suit.